Sustainability is for Everyone

Alan AtKisson

An ISIS ACADEMY publication

Sustainability is for Everyone

First edition 2013

An ISIS Academy publication
www.ISISAcademy.com

ISBN: 0991102207
ISBN-13: 978-0991102204

DEDICATION

In memory of Donella Meadows,

whom I was lucky enough

to befriend

CONTENTS

Before we begin …

Imagine that you have a childhood friend with whom you kept in contact into your adult years. You had great affection for each other in childhood, so it bothered you when this friend began smoking. Later you noticed that your friend was smoking more, and also drinking more alcohol. Lately, your friend has also developed a bad gambling habit, and has asked to borrow money from you. You can see the trend in your friend's life: things cannot go on this way. Either health, or personal economy, or family will eventually reach a breaking point. The results will be tragic. So you want somehow to intervene. You want to help this friend change direction, and live a more healthy, happy, and balanced life.

In a word, you want your friend's life to become more *sustainable*.

For this is what sustainability means, at its most basic level: a way of life — for individual people, families, communities, companies, nations, even our whole global civilization — that does *not* seem inevitably destined for a crash. A way of life where our needs and wants as human beings, and nature's needs for care and balance, are not in conflict with each other. A way of life where our resources are managed well, and the big, obvious risks are avoided. A way of life that can continue for generations, providing everyone on this Earth with a chance to enjoy a good life, while contributing to the greater good.

This is the sustainability vision in a nutshell. People who work for sustainability — whether they are professionals in the field, or simply dedicated to making positive change, whatever profession they follow — usually feel something like the person described above, who wants to help a friend find a better life. Because allowing dangerous trends to run their course, without intervention, is simply unthinkable.

If you also feel this way, even a tiny bit, then this book is for you.

About this book

The purpose of this little book is to inspire you.

I have been working professionally in sustainability for 25 years. That is a long time, and I have worked hard during that time to promote the vision and the practice of sustainability. I have given hundreds of speeches, presentations and workshops, in 44 countries; created tools and methods for spreading sustainability (tools which have themselves spread into many countries); trained hundreds of other sustainability professionals and change agents (to help them spread sustainability); published books and articles; and consulted to large companies, governments, cities, NGOs, and the United Nations. I have even written songs about sustainability.

In 2013, I was elected into the Sustainability Hall of Fame™, by the International Society of Sustainability Professionals.[1]

To mark the occasion — because the event organizers asked me to "share some wisdom" from my experience — I wrote this small book. In reality, the book is an essay, a word originally meaning "attempt". Partly, I am attempting to make up for the fact that I do not really feel worthy of such distinctions. Yes, I have worked hard, but there is so much more that needs to be done; others have worked harder. Also, this book is an attempt to say a few things about sustainability — its past, present, and future — that do not fit well into other forms of writing. The first-person essay allows one to mix thoughts and feelings,

---

[1] I was very touched and honored by this distinction — though I must note that the phrase "sustainability hall of fame" seems almost an oxymoron. If one works in sustainability, one is anything *but* famous. But I deeply thank the jury of the ISSP for placing me in the company of other people whose work and life-examples have been inspirations to me; and I acknowledge, gratefully, that I would never have received this distinction had I not been mentored, coached, and befriended by some of the most brilliant sustainability minds on the planet, especially the founders and members of the Balaton Group.

reflections and advice, in a very personal way, which is perfect for what I have to say.

The essay is also a good place to share some warnings and regrets.

Why would I write about warnings and regrets, in an essay-book intended to inspire you? Because I have encountered a few situations in my professional life that were troublesome, and I would like to help you — as an aspiring or experienced sustainability worker — to avoid such trouble yourself. I want to share some insights that have helped me along the way, but I also want you to learn from my mistakes; for in fact, there is usually more learning in failure than in success.

Mostly, I want to get a specific message across, and I want to ask you to help me spread that message.

Here is the principal message of this book:

Sustainability is for everyone.

This is a simple statement, but it has profound implications. For the past several decades, sustainability — and many other words and concepts that are attached to it — has been the hearth fire for a relatively small but highly engaged group of professional researchers, managers, activists, teachers, and consultants. And since the phrase "sustainable development" was first formally introduced to the world in 1987, by a United Nations commission chaired by Norway's then-prime minister Gro Harlem Brundtland, it has slowly gathered more and more people around that fire.

When "old-timers" like me look around, we get a wonderful feeling, because there are so many more of us now, all gathered around that beautiful, idealistic flame. Compared to the "old days," the gathering now seems truly enormous.

But the growth of this special gathering is also a problem. For sustainability should not be something that is set apart, something that only special, highly engaged people can understand, talk about, work with. Sustainability is not a secret knowledge.

Sustainability is for everyone.

Sustainability means making the world work. For everyone. And that means that it is time for us to leave this special gathering, take this wonderful flame of sustainability, and carry it into the world.

And take it with us everywhere.

This book sets forward a few ideas and suggestions for how to make sustainability more universally accessible, without watering it down or changing its meaning. The book is meant to start a conversation, and to help further accelerate a trend that is already happening: the normalization of sustainability thinking and practice into every area of life.

For those of us who are sustainability workers, that is our ultimate goal. Looking backward, we have come a long distance. Looking forward, we have far to go, and there remain many obstacles in our path. Chief among these is the fact that sustainability itself is still not easy to communicate — and not everyone knows they need it.

But as more and more people know, or at least feel, they *do* need it. The whole world needs sustainability, and fast. So here are some thoughts about how to overcome that obstacle and take sustainability more effectively into those places where it is most needed.

We have to make sustainability something that is not just for us — the people who identify themselves as "sustainability people" — but for everyone.

What sustainability brings to the party

If the world were a party, sustainability would be the smart-but-nerdy cousin who somehow does not get invited — not because nobody likes her, but because everyone assumes that she will not fit in. Or that she does not *like* to party. Or that she does not know how.

But if everyone understood what sustainability actually has to offer, she would be invited to *every* party, because she would be so much fun and bring so much value.

Indeed, sustainability should be nothing less than the *life of the party*. After all, without sustainability, the party could become a deadly nightmare.

So let's take a look at a few things that sustainability work has going for it, in generic content terms. When we do, we will see that these are things that should have great value to almost any professional person, manager, manufacturing company, teacher, government agency, you-name-it.

When people see the value they gain from these elements of sustainability work, engagement with sustainability itself will eventually follow.

A systems perspective. Goodness knows, in this complex, interconnected world, everyone needs to have a system perspective. Systems literacy — understanding the basics of stocks, flows, feedback loops, delays, together with the interplay between human choice and the web of physical and social ripple effects that follow from our decisions — should be a universal educational requirement. (Tip: Read Donella Meadows' classic book *Thinking in Systems: A Primer*, Chelsea Green, 2008. Her writing on systems is always the best place to start.)

What Sustainability brings to the Party!

The phrase "systems thinking" sounds complicated, but it is actually quite fun. In fact, there are a lot of excellent games about systems thinking that you can use at school, at work ... but also at a party! See *The Systems Thinking Playbook.*[2]

_____

[2] *The Systems Thinking Playbook*, by Linda Booth Sweeney and Dennis Meadows, published by Chelsea Green, 2008. These wonderful teaching games are easy to learn, and to lead ... and they really will work at a party!

Besides, having a systems perspective brings nothing less than joy, because it creates endless sources of intellectual pleasure.[3] Asking "And what causes that?" or "What impact does that have?" can lead one down endless trails of discovery and understanding.

Long-term thinking. "Thinking" here is not a loose, fluffy word. Long-term thinking involves the ability to read trends, analyze data, strategize, and plan for preferred outcomes. Hooray for thinking! Sustainability brings loads of it onto the dance floor, and builds everyone's capacity to grapple with tough problems of any kind. Big value!

A New Compass. Sustainability helps people grapple with environmental quality, economic productivity, social and governance issues of many stripes, and human wellbeing, all at the same time. Many years ago, it struck me that these four dimensions of sustainability (originally identified by Herman Daly, see below) mapped nicely onto a compass: N=Nature, E=Economy, S=Society, and W=Wellbeing. Since its invention in 1997, the Sustainability Compass has spread around the

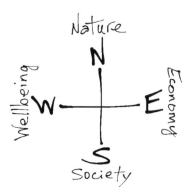

world, from aboriginal communities in Australia and Latin America, to schools in the Philippines and Thailand, to the offices of corporate executives in Europe and the United States. What a conversation piece! Bring the Sustainability Compass to *your* next party. Or workshop, or board meeting, or curriculum planning session.

A sense of meaning and purpose. I believe that many people work without any sense that their work contributes to a worthy, long-term purpose. If I am right, and sustainability really is for everyone, then

---

[3] I believe that intellectual pleasure is part of partying. Sure, people drink and dance and carry on with each other at parties. But they also talk. They hole up in corners and share their deepest thoughts and secrets. They go outside, look up at the Milky Way and say, "oh, wow!" The party metaphor works fine here.

everyone can share in the sense of importance and significance that striving for sustainability brings to any job or profession, and not just to sustainability professionals. This opportunity for a feeling of meaning should not be framed in ways that create feelings of specialness and separateness, however. There are many ways, rather ordinary ways, that sustainability can bring a sense of purpose to one's work, from "I'm making the world a better place for my children," to "I'm working to protect something I really care about," to "I believe in fairness and in giving everyone an equal chance at achieving success in life." These thoughts and their associated feelings scratch deeper itches within us than "I am helping to maximize value for our shareholders." Working for sustainability gives people the chance to have such thoughts every day.

I bet you can improve this list of what sustainability brings to the party, starting with the obvious practical things I left out (such as cost saving, risk reduction, and innovation), stretching as far as an understanding of your own favorite abstract-global concept. (My current favorite-new-concept is the new name given to our geological era, when humans became the dominant force for change on planet Earth: "Anthropocene."[4])

Sustainability is for everyone because everyone can find something useful or fascinating in the family of concepts, tools, and practices that actually make up sustainability work. If they become familiar with these concepts, tools, and practices, and start using them, they will very probably find something of great value — to themselves, to their organization, to their community and nation, and certainly to the world at large.

---

[4] Here is a beautiful and informative website that explains this new concept: http://www.anthropocene.info

Sustainability, Big and Small

One of the founders of sustainable development thinking is Herman Daly, the great ecological economist. Daly's work introduced me to many new ideas and concepts — ideas that have become so common and integrated into sustainability that professionals scarcely notice them anymore. Among many other contributions (including the four categories that became the Sustainability Compass), Daly introduced me to the concept of weak and strong sustainability. In fact, "weak sustainability" is probably not sustainable at all: it relies on continuously substituting nature's resources, as they run out or get scarce, with human ingenuity. That does happen to some extent, but the idea of "weak sustainability" does not fully take nature's non-negotiable boundaries into account. We really do have just one planet, and must live within its limits, which is the realization behind "strong sustainability" — the concept I prefer. (As did Daly.)[5]

But reading Herman Daly's work also introduced me to the idea that there can be more than one kind of sustainability, and that making these distinctions can help us talk and think about the idea more clearly. In that spirit, I would like to introduce two *new* concepts: big and small sustainability.

"Big sustainability" refers to the great challenges that all of us working on sustainability must grapple with: climate change, biodiversity loss, lifting billions of people to higher levels of material well-being, and so

---

[5] Here are some formal definitions, adapted from those I learned from Herman Daly and others: practicing "weak sustainability" means that one accepts the depletion of natural capital, because one believes that manufactured capital can always take its place. Adopting "strong sustainability" means that one believes that manufactured capital cannot endlessly be substituted for natural capital, and that stocks of natural capital must be maintained or enhanced.

on. We sometimes refer to this as "global sustainability."

"Small sustainability" means the kinds of things that sustainability workers are usually working on – for example, the wellbeing of a specific school, or the internal strategies of a medium-size company to change their production produces and reduce their environmental impact.

Obviously these two concepts are deeply related: small sustainability issues are *issues* because of the big sustainability challenges with which we are faced. However, in practical terms, it is very important to know *which of these two concepts you are working on at the moment.*

When communicating with people about matters related to the "S" word, stop and ask yourself, is my task here to engage people on a big sustainability matter? Do I need to bring them up to speed on the latest climate science, or the news about the most recent animal to appear on the endangered species list, or the status of rich and poor in the world? That's big sustainability.

Or do I actually need to focus my attention and intention on helping this particular person, or this particular organization, take a solid step in the direction of an incrementally better world? Help them make their next and best contribution? That's small sustainability.

The distinctions here are not so blindingly obvious as they appear at first glance. In fact, many people working on sustainability often get them confused. Many of us engage with a group on a small sustainability issue ... but then try to stuff big sustainability into it. We keep thinking globally, when we really should just focus on acting locally. (This is a tendency I routinely have to struggle with myself.)

Sustainability for everyone ultimately means both big *and* small. But as we will see, small sustainability is usually the more important and effective place to start.

Small sustainability is *especially* for everyone.

How do you talk to a _____ about sustainability?

You can fill in the blank above. And in that blank, you can put any type of person or organizational role you want. The answer to this question will always be the same.

In their own language.

Do you need to talk to a Chief Financial Officer? Be ready with the numbers and case studies showing positive return on investment and avoidance of risk. Fortunately, there is plenty of that sort of information already available, and legions of consultants and NGOs are creating more of it all the time.

A teacher? Well, there is a rich vocabulary and community of practice called "Education for Sustainable Development," with a well-developed pedagogy and a global movement that was even given its own UN "Decade" (2005-2014). (Confession: I never once used the word "pedagogy" until I started working with sustainability educators. Now, I often use that word, even though I find it a bit ugly. Sometimes you have to adopt the local language in order to speak with the natives.)

How about a safety expert? Sustainability is about safety in the long term, and many traditional safety issues — workplace accidents, hazardous waste management — are also sustainability issues. Acknowledging this prominently, from the beginning, helps build a bridge to other issues such as reducing impact on natural systems, minimizing vulnerability to climate change, and more. (This approach worked very well for me recently, once when I was consulting to a construction company, and then again with a group of industrial transportation experts.)

Those three were relatively easy. Can you talk to a hockey player about sustainability? Hockey players are tough, but nobody lasts in that game if they do not take care of themselves and think long-term. The action involves lots of passing and ricocheting, which reminds one of a system's complexity. Sustainability, like hockey, helps people collaborate, innovate, and find new pathways through tough obstacles, to reach ambitious goals. Plus, there is that whole thing about trying to keep the ice from melting ...

See what I mean? All it takes is a little thinking about the context in which that person works, and you can easily start a meaningful conversation about sustainability issues and themes.

Obviously, you need to be a bit skillful here — and I mean skillful at the art of conversation. If you meet a hockey player at a party, you do not say, "Oh! You're a hockey player! Ha ha, let's talk about global warming and melting arctic ice ... " If you do that, you are lucky if the hockey player just walks away, instead of smacking you.

But if you start a nice, normal conversation, then that joke about global warming and melting ice might just come up naturally — and maybe from the hockey player herself.

While speaking the person's professional language is a good way to *start* a conversation, by all means, don't stop there. Especially once you have gotten to know that person on a human level, it is not a big leap to start talking about human things: general concerns about the future, the state of nature, the kind of society or planet our children will inherit. In my experience, even the crustiest, rightward-leaning global warming skeptic has a soft spot around points like this. With most such people, you can even find larger points of commonality in connection with the long-term, whole-system concerns that epitomize sustainability at its essence. You just have to look.

(In fact, some of my favorite professional memories involve watching people of this description get that part-worried, part-aha expression that comes with discovering that they actually have something in common with the green-tinged people they previously so despised.)

It is much easier to get almost anyone talking about sustainability these days, because so many *other* people are talking about it. Even the World Economic Forum, perhaps the most power-dense gathering on the planet, grapples with issues of sustainability at its annual meetings.[6]

So, do not let the apparent distance from sustainability to the person or profession in question stop you. There are always ways to bring sustainability into the conversation — and this is the first step toward bringing sustainability into everyone's professional work and daily life.

---

[6] The World Economic Forum's 2013 meeting focused special attention on sustainability and related concepts such as resilience. See one thread here:
http://www.weforum.org/issues/sustainability

How *not* to talk about sustainability

Sometimes, in order to talk effectively about sustainability, you have to not use that word.

This is hard: when you are passionate about something (and most people who work in this field are passionate about it), you want to talk about it. But people react in funny ways to some words, and "sustainability" is one of them.

So what do you do when the person you are talking to is a known skeptic, critic, or even enemy of sustainability? (Yes, unfortunately, sustainability has enemies.)

You just use other words.

For example, in a business context, you can always turn to the usual organizational synonyms, such as "Corporate Social Responsibility" or "Ethical Business." You can pepper your speech with phrases like "value-added" and "stakeholder relations." Anyone working in the field quickly learns how to do this.

But in more challenging situations, where people exhibit active animosity to sustainability, you have a choice to make. You can rise to sustainability's defense ... or you just talk about sustainability without using the word. Here are some examples:

"Well, if we keep on going in this direction, we are going to run into some serious problems. We have to find some new, longer-term options. What would you suggest?"

"Looks to me like your supply chain is pretty vulnerable to environmental disturbances. What are you planning to do about that?"

"I've been reading some very interesting studies that show how happiness and wellbeing are correlated with greater productivity and even profitability."

See that? I never once said the "S" word.

But there are other strategies available to you, besides just banning sustainability from your vocabulary for a time.

"Take-out sustainability"

Let's assume that you have gotten over the hurdle regarding whether to use, or not use, the word "sustainability." You are in a conversation with someone, or even with a whole group.

What should you talk about?

Let's assume further that not everyone wants to know everything about climate change, energy transformations, living within the Planetary Boundaries, declining biodiversity, eliminating poverty and the like. Fair assumption, yes?

And yet, when we work on sustainability we often assume nearly the opposite. We assume that everyone needs to know everything, right now, and we start talking about it.

We make the "big sustainability" mistake.

This is like inviting someone to a nice meal, and then immediately informing him or her that it will be a banquet of 27 courses — many of which are new to this person, and not all of them easy to eat. No wonder many people just don't bother to show up.

So let's talk about another strategy for avoiding this problem. The strategy is called, "take-out sustainability."

Yes, I have jumped into food metaphors. I am comparing, for example, some yummy Chinese take-out noodles to that inedible 27-course banquet: the noodles are much easier to eat. But there is another layer of meaning here: "take-out sustainability" means picking one aspect of sustainability work, and taking it out of the sustainability context.

(I know, this feels wrong, sustainability is all about context. Please bear with me a minute.)

Take, for example, systems thinking. If you want to approach someone for whom sustainability-the-banquet is just too much, you can try just introducing them to the take-out dish called systems thinking. "Look," you might say, "here's an approach to problem analysis that might help you." Show them how a little dab of systems thinking helps them solve a real problem that they have — whatever it is.

Don't say a word about greenhouse gases, ecosystem limits, or global equity at this stage! Just get them comfortable with this one aspect of a sustainability approach. Show them its value. Show them that it works. Get them used to making new connections that they have not seen before. Then, sooner or later, you can say, "well you know, systems thinking is really at the heart of that sustainability stuff you might have been hearing about."

Or take wellbeing: you might introduce an organization to the rise of wellbeing (or happiness, depending on who you are talking to) as a new way of measuring progress. Improving performance. Attracting talent. Whatever the most convincing argument is for that person, and for that concept.

Then, once you have them hooked on W for Wellbeing, you can introduce them to the rest of the picture, in simple terms: "You know, Wellbeing is just one part of this very useful tool called the Sustainability Compass: W stands for Wellbeing, instead of West. Then N is for Nature, E for Economy, S for Society and social concerns." (You don't have to use the Compass, of course. If you have another preferred framework, just substitute that here.)

Or maybe the smart thing to do will be to stay with Wellbeing (or systems thinking, or whatever take-out dish you have selected) for a good long while. Here's the thing: since everything really is connected, these take-out dishes will eventually pull in the rest of sustainability.

Sooner or later, the wellbeing of workers links up with environmental threats. The general application of systems thinking gradually forces a confrontation with resource constraints. The process may feel slow, but take-out sustainability is an effective strategy, because the system linkages involved must ultimately exert their force, almost like gravity. Physicists consider gravity a very weak force (it takes the whole Earth just to hold you down!), but it is, after all, quite inevitable — as is sustainability. And slow sustainability is much better than no sustainability at all.

Your objective, in using this strategy, is just to get people interested in one "take-out dish." Once you do that and establish a relationship (or, if you already know this person or organization, establish a new dimension in your existing relationship), and you prove that this dish is tasty ... then you can introduce another dish. And another.

And at the right moment you might say, "you know, all of these tools and approaches and perspectives we have been talking about are all part of doing sustainability."

But remember: don't get impatient and suddenly drag them up to the banquet table, unless they really seem to be asking for it. Keep bringing useful, tasty "sustainability dishes" to *their* table. Keep it easy: just as take-out meals always come with their own forks, napkins, and condiments, make sure this person's interaction with sustainability is as frictionless as possible. Bring tools, case studies, and inspiring stories.

Sustainability is an acquired taste. But it is a taste than nearly everyone can acquire, if you give them a step-by-step path.

Sustainability = Quality

Something like fifteen years ago, I made a bold claim. Someday, I said, sustainability will be like quality and the sustainability movement will be like TQM. Remember TQM? "Total Quality Management"? No, many people reading this will not remember the quality movement. (And many of you reading this will probably have to search for that term, TQM, on the Internet.)

That's because doing manufacturing with a serious attention to quality has long ago ceased to be a novel issue. There is no need for a missionary-style "quality movement" anymore. Setting high quality standards in manufacturing, aiming for zero defects in your products, used to be a bold new idea. Now, it is absolutely normal.

"And that is what will happen to sustainability in the future," I used to say, to anyone who would listen. "Sustainability will become the new normal."

Now we are in that future. And in fact, that is exactly what has long since begun to happen.

In becoming more normal, sustainability has followed a similar, well-trodden path, graduating from the incubator stage of think-tanks and activists, through early adoption by visionaries and market leaders, to standardization and rigorous planning routines in governments, large corporations, and institutions.

In this way, sustainability is already *just like* quality.

So it is time to make a new, bolder prediction: *sustainability and quality will merge.* They will become the same thing.

With this statement, I do not mean that sustainability will be subsumed into highly structured Lean Six Sigma quality management programs (though that integration is happening too[7]). I mean that sustainability will come to be seen as a basic criteria of ... well, everything related to making a product or providing a service. Of course we should make things well and do things well. That is quality. And doing things well includes doing them sustainably. So sustainability is — or at least soon will be — part of quality too.

In the not-so-distant future, things that are not sustainable will come to be seen as shabby, tasteless, unattractive, unskilled, and boorish. Lacking quality.

---

[7] Here is a recent (Mar 2013) article that describes the Lean Six Sigma management system and its growing relationship to sustainability:
http://www.greenbiz.com/blog/2013/03/01/sustainability-close-business-usual

Do I mean really mean everything? Yes, everything.

Take football: either the American version, or the Australian version ("footy"), or the rest of the world's version ("soccer"). We all know what quality football entails. Right now, "a quality football game" does not include sustainability, or at least not much.

But it easily could. From the team uniforms to the way teams travel, from the food served at the stadium (and the stadium itself) to the social impact of the sport and the way the economics are handled, it is easy to imagine *many* more sustainable ways of doing all those things.

Indeed, it is nearly inevitable that someday, they *will* be done much more sustainably.

And *not* doing them in a sustainable way will be seen as shabby, tasteless, unattractive, unskilled, and boorish. Just as a football player had better make sure those socks are pulled up before running out onto the field of the championship game, the stadium staff will make sure that the grass was prepared with solar-powered machinery, and that food served at the match all comes from healthy, sustainable sources, in compostable containers (or some higher-tech solution that is truly part of a circular economy). The players will arrive in carbon-neutral vehicles, and the owners will notice the positive impact of sustainability on their bottom line. Soon, to do anything less will be considered way behind the times. (Oh, wait a minute: this is already happening, in the US National Football League.[8])

To repeat — because this is really important — sustainability is becoming an extension of how we think about quality, *in general terms*. Things that are not sustainable will not qualify to be called "good," "high quality," or "well-made." That reality is not here yet ... but it is

---

[8] After drafting that section on football (and not before), I searched the Internet for the phrase "football sustainability." Up came an article just one week old about how the NFL in the US is embracing sustainability, in just this way:
http://www.guardian.co.uk/sustainable-business/nfl-champion-sustainability

just around the corner.

One way of practicing "Sustainability is for everyone" is to put yourself in that future time, when sustainability = quality. Wherever you go, look around. What do you see that is not good, yet … but that will be, someday?

Who can you engage in starting to make that vision real?

Where do you see an opportunity for sustainability, just waiting to happen?

Sustainability and resilience

I digress for a moment to lay one worry to rest: sustainability is not on the way out. Lately it has been fashionable, in some circles, to say that sustainability is "over" and that resilience is taking its place. At least, the author of one popular recent book about resilience has made claims like this.[9]

Here's the thing: others have made similar statements before, about sustainability not being a good-enough term, or about other concepts replacing sustainability. Others have claimed that sustainability was just too boring, or complicated, or vague to be useful. (How something can be both complicated and vague at the same time is a mystery to me, but I have heard people use both criticisms in the same breath.)

This kind of occasional, critical talk has been going on for years. And sustainability is still here.

Here's the other thing: few people who actually study resilience scientifically would support the claim that resilience can replace sustainability — because they are two very different concepts. In fact, resilience is a *part of* sustainability.

Resilience is a wonderful, useful, critically important idea. It is essential to sustainability. Unless things can withstand shocks, "bounce back," change and adapt to changing circumstances, they will not be ... sustainable.

But there are other dimensions of sustainability that have nothing to do with resilience. A community can be resilient, but still be destroyed by a

---

[9] Andrew Zolli, "Learning to Bounce Back," *New York Times,* 2 Nov 2012
http://www.nytimes.com/2012/11/03/opinion/forget-sustainability-its-about-resilience.html

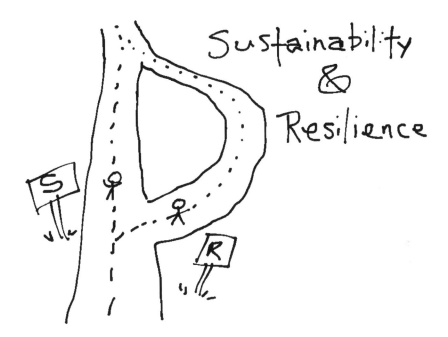

nuclear disaster, for example. By all means, adopt resilience, use that term, wherever the concept is appropriate. If people prefer to talk about resilience, by all means do that. (See "How not to talk about sustainability," above.)

But do not be fooled yourself. Sustainability, the word, may wax and wane in popularity and use. But sustainability, the concept, is not going away. We are always going to have to deal with long-term, systemic issues of continuance — until and unless we become so deeply and automatically sustainable as a civilization that we really no longer need to think about it at all.

I look forward to that day, but it is not here yet.

The burden of knowledge

One of the great occupational hazards of working in sustainability is the obligation to keep oneself well informed about the state of the world.

This part of the work is usually not fun. Or rather, it is *mostly* not fun. Yes, there can be a certain ghoulish fascination some of us feel when reading about what runaway climate change would do to human civilization, or when watching a new clip on the demise of a species. But the feeling that we are watching some thrilling planetary-level catastrophe film, or a global murder mystery, wears off quickly. This is reality, not fantasy. One soon becomes glum, and wishes the bad news would just stop.

For example, as I was writing this chapter, news arrived that the average level of carbon dioxide in the atmosphere was about to cross the 400 parts per million barrier — higher than it has ever been so long as modern humans have existed. Global emissions greenhouse gases are actually following the "worst case scenario" curves of previous climate assessments. We may wake up, just a few years from now, to a world where the arctic sea ice disappears completely each summer. We are on track to create a very hot world.

I know this ... and I am not happy about knowing it. Such knowledge feels like a big, overloaded backpack, pulling down on my shoulders and slowing my step.

How does one deal with this burden of being extra well-informed about these unrelenting, soul-crushing threats to life as we know it, and the apparently dimming prospects of attaining the brighter future we all hope for?

There are only three ways that I have ever found that worked.

One: commiserating with friends. I love that word "commiserate" — to "miserate" together. Misery truly does love company. And there truly is misery in knowing that we may soon see the last of the wild tigers, or that millions are already suffering the life-or-death impacts of climate change. There is no getting easily around the emotions that arise naturally in connection with such knowledge. So get together with other people, and let the woe out. Some do this over beer, some do it in religious or ceremonial ways, each according to his or her culture. However you choose to do it, do it. Expressing a bit of that grief, fear, anger, and despair will do you a surprising amount of good. Feeling bad, together with other people, actually helps you feel better.

Two: humor. As I wrote in *Believing Cassandra*, when I first began to work professionally on serious global problems such as global warming, writing darkly humorous songs about the quandaries of our time helped me to put down that backpack for a while, and lighten my own sense of burden. You don't need to write your own songs or make your own jokes to let humor do its magic. Just find somebody who is good at such things, and let them make you laugh. It is best to do this with other people as well: absurdity loves company, too.

Three — and this is really the most important one, of course — cultivate hope. How do you do that? Simple: by taking action.

None of these big sustainability problems, about which we all know too much, will get solved unless we all keep working at solving them. Said positively, they *all* get solved if we *all* get busy, take action, and work hard, for a long time, on things both big and small.

Let me share with you one of my own current actions, which I am taking now, with the intent of cultivating hope, and lightening my own sense of burden in knowing too much, for too long, about unsustainable trends on this planet:

Sustainability is for everyone.

"Doing" sustainability

"Yes, but what do I *do?*"

Almost everyone who works on sustainability, and who tries to engage other people to work on sustainability, must respond to this question (or variations on it) very often.

Whether sustainability is "big" or "small," the word almost always sounds abstract. That is because it *is* abstract. Sustainability is a concept, a way of thinking, a way of analyzing and understanding.

So what does it mean to *do* sustainability? How do we answer this question?

That depends.

First, it depends on the situation of the person asking the question. For a CEO, considerations of sustainability lead to certain decisions that need to be made, and often certain change processes. "Let's reduce our carbon emissions from fossil fuel use," for example. Or, "I've been reviewing the recent management literature on how fostering greater happiness and wellbeing improves performance at work, and I think we need to make some changes in how we treat our workers."

For an ordinary householder, the topics might sound similar, but the content changes. "What kind of car should I buy? Given the fact that I want to reduce my carbon emissions, should I even buy a car?" Or, "How can I improve my happiness and wellbeing at work?"

In general, *doing* sustainability, just like talking about it, depends a great deal on *who* is doing it, and in what situation.

Is it always a good idea to embrace vegetarian eating, for example? Not if you are an Inuit hunter. What about driving less? This would be exceedingly difficult for a forestry worker, who commutes to a patch of land far away each morning.

There is no simple way around this fact: decisions about how to "do sustainability" are always *context-dependent*. There is no universal "Ten Things You Can Do" list that applies to everyone.

There are only questions to ask ... and then, decisions and actions to take, depending on the answers to those questions.

Here is a simple set of questions that you can use with yourself, or with others, to get started. They might help you find good answers to that perplexing, big question we started with: "What do I do?"

1. What trends do I see around me that are not sustainable?

What situations do you see that really cannot continue as they are, without leading inevitably to serious problems down the road, for people, nature, or both? Just look: you will see many of them.

2. Which of these trends do I want to work on changing?

That phase "want to" is very important here. There are *many* problems that fall under the category of "sustainability problems." No one can do everything. But everyone can do something, and the best way to sustain your own energy is to choose something where you feel a personal motivation. Having that feeling of "want to," instead of "have to," will help you *continue* doing something, over the long term.

3. What decisions and actions can I take to create positive change?

Again, the important phrase is "can I take". Everyone can make decisions about their own choices, their own behavior. Everyone can do their best to "walk their talk" — to demonstrate in their personal lives the changes they wish to see around them.

But most of us can also take decisions and actions that influence other people, or even whole organizations. We *can* choose different policies, different goals, different practices, different ways of measuring our success. The ultimate question is really this one: Will we do it?

"Doing" sustainability is all about turning "can" into "will". The only person who can do that for you … is you.

Against "sustainable consumption"

Usually I defend the language of sustainability against all attackers. Now, however, I am going to be critical. There is one phrase that we really should change in our common language of sustainability. It will be hard to change, because the phrase is enshrined in international agreements, in the names of organizations, and in millions of minds.

We need to stop talking about "sustainable consumption". We need to stop thinking of people as "sustainable consumers."

The problem is with the word "consume." It means, "to destroy."

Consumers are destroyers. We do not need "sustainable destroyers." We need people who use sustainable products and services, in a sustainable way: with the long-term, and the whole system, in mind.

Here is a suggestion to businesses: Drop consumer. Bring back the word "customer". Customers are people who have the custom, the habit, of coming back to you again and again. The phrase "sustainable customer" is nearly redundant! Good customers have, by definition, a sustainable, long-term relationship with your business.

Finding new, sustainable business models is as simple (and as difficult) as moving from the model of "consumer" back to "customer."

And as for "sustainable consumption": please avoid this oxymoron. Try using "sustainable use."

Then, keep using that phrase, over and over. Just as you might reuse a sustainable product.

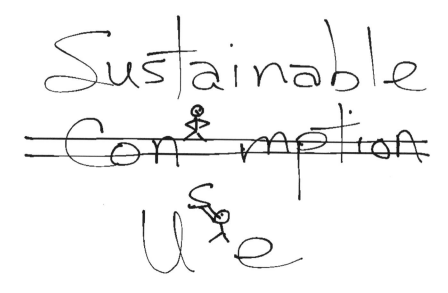

(Note: In keeping with earlier advice, here is a caveat. If you work with people who really like to use "sustainable consumption," or who must use it for some reason, there is no need to argue about it. Even if you share my view, just note their preference. Speak their language ... and move on to doing the real work of making positive change.)

Sustainability and optimism

A few years ago, I heard someone in a seminar audience ask the great global-systems researcher Lester Brown this question: "After all these years of watching global environmental trends get worse, how do you maintain your optimism?" Lester's reply was immediate. "I have a one-word answer for that: bourbon."

Later, I used to borrow Lester's one-liner (with attribution) and change the ending to a two-word answer: single malt.

Of course, Lester was (mostly) joking, for he went on to talk about looking for, and seeing, signs of change all around us.

And now I have mostly abandoned "single malt" as a laugh line, and adopted a different set of one- and two-word answers that speak more seriously to the question of how to maintain a sense of optimism. Here are a few of them:

Children. Whether you have children (I do), or you just know and love other people's children (I do that too), children can be a great source of optimism. The older you get, the more they look like enormous bundles of possibility. They are also walking, talking emissaries to the future: by the time they arrive at the future, they will be enormously skilled at dealing with problems that neither you nor I can even imagine. With so much future possibility walking around, such clear evidence that the reinforcements are on their way, it is hard *not* to believe that sustainability work will continue, and that the world will witness ever-increasing, ever-accelerating positive change.

Innovation. Just look around! We are awash with innovation! Who would have thought, ten years ago, that Germany would now be covered in solar electricity panels? How did all these city-bike and car-share systems spring up so fast? Look what's happened to light bulbs, for goodness sake! Change is definitely happening fast, and much of it is very promising. The accelerating presence of innovation in our lives is a great encouragement; we just need to turn more and more of it in a sustainable direction.

Human history. Shakespeare gives Hamlet a great phrase: "the slings and arrows of outrageous fortune." Humans have certainly experienced their fair share of *those* over the centuries and millennia. Ice ages could have wiped us out, not to mention outrageous plagues, wars, and planet-shadowing volcanic eruptions. We are still here. Human history is *already* a story of big challenges followed by adaptation, invention, and survival, sometimes against very tough "slings and arrows." We've made it before; we'll make it again.

Recent history. This one is more personal: during more than two decades of sustainability work, I have seen many things change for the better — including very fundamental things. I remember when nobody I met had ever heard of sustainability. I remember when even my own family members just scratched their heads and kept asking me, "uh, what is it you do again?" Now, they are all engaged with sustainability, at least personally. Now most people I meet, at least in professional life, know what sustainability is — and most big organizations even have sustainability officers. We have come a long way. Optimism for the future comes from seeing, and remembering, the progress of the past.

Music. This is my favorite one-word answer these days to the optimism question. Music has been an absolutely reliable constant in my life, providing me with solace in moments of despair, elation in moments of celebration, and a creative outlet when things around me felt destructive. Not everyone makes music, or even likes music. But everyone can find that "something" (hobby, art, sport, recreational activity of any kind) that is a joy unto itself — and an engine of continuance during those times when you just feel like just stopping.

Whatever you do, please don't stop. We need you.

Maintaining optimism is essential to not stopping. But optimism is not a character trait. It is a choice, and it requires constant cultivation. You have to find your own "one- or two-word answer" to the question I heard posed to Lester Brown (and have had posed to me countless times). Find it. Do it.

And remember that there are always unexpected encouragements waiting just around the bend. You can count on it.

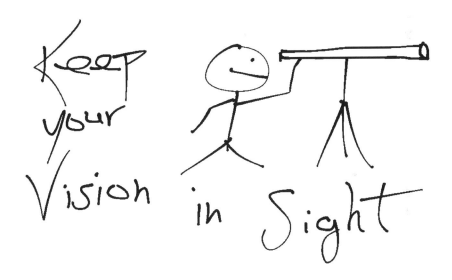

Invisible sustainability

There are many ways that sustainability, in all its dimensions, is already present around us. We often do not see it very clearly, or at all, because it is too remote, too incremental, too under-reported. I consider myself very well informed, but I am regularly surprised by the sudden appearance of previously invisible sustainability. I have come to the point that I now take it for granted that there is much more sustainability happening than I can see.

For example, during a recent work visit to the beautiful country of Namibia, in southern Africa, I chanced to meet up with a friend-of-a-friend, a man named Keith, who works for WWF. Over a glass of fantastic South African wine, Keith told me the amazing story of how Namibia set about to create community-based conservation councils in the late 1990s. These councils have thrived and multiplied to the point where one in eight Namibians participates in them. Namibia, as a direct result, has rapidly *growing* populations of lion, elephant, mountain zebra and more — together with growing tourism revenues, and improvements in resulting quality of life for its poorer citizens.

That's sustainable development — movement towards sustainability — at its very best: large-scale, rapid change that creates positives at all the points of the Compass. Nature is healing. The Economy is bustling. The Social fabric is getting enriched. And the Wellbeing of people is definitely improving.

And this whole story was completely invisible to me until a few weeks ago. (Thanks, Keith Sproule!)

Maybe you already knew the Namibia story, and maybe you did not. In any case, I will bet you dollars to donuts that there are a thousand other

Sustainability is there ...
if you just know how to
see it

sustainability stories like that out there in the world, even out there in your own community, that you do not know about already.

And if you learn about them, you will feel compelled to share the best of them with others (as I felt compelled to tell you about Namibia), because they cultivate hope and inspire action.

So to inspire *you* to keep looking for "invisible sustainability," I will give you a little blank box. Go do some poking around. Find something wonderful happening in sustainability that you did not already know about, that too few people know about.

Then write it in here. Make the invisible visible.

A few things to watch out for

At a party, people sometimes let their hair down and reveal things about the way they really think — things that they might not talk about in a professional meeting. This is one of those moments.

I promised that I would write about regrets and warnings with regard to sustainability work, and here they are. They are not many. For now, I want to focus on three of the most important ones. At least, they were important lessons for me.

First, I regret those times when I brought my guitar along on a business trip, but never took the guitar out of the case. I probably watched a bad movie on the hotel television, instead of making a bit of music — which, as I have recently explained, I can always rely on for a psychological boost or balm.

I am not suggesting that you should play the guitar. For me, this regret is about something deeply symbolic that applies to all of us. Often, we have what we really need with us. It's right there. We would feel so much better, or be so much more productive, if we just used the knowledge, the tools, and the insights from experience that we already have, right at hand. These things are like me and my guitar: too often, we don't even take them out of the case.

Second, I want to share a warning with you. There have been a few times in my professional life when I did not recognize a power play or a piece of sabotage coming before it actually hit me. When something like that does hit you — when you finally see that someone has been working behind the scenes to redirect the course of events, or sabotage your initiative, or undermine you as the driver of change — it is too late. You are caught up in a maelstrom of action and reaction, and often it is too much work just to deal with the emotional side of what is happening. It rarely turns out well.

But there are ways to recognize these things before they hit; one learns them with hindsight, of course, but one can also learn to read the signs, with foresight. And when you do see these signs even a little bit in advance, you can work with your emotions first, set them aside, think strategically as well as compassionately, and find a way to avoid the storm before it hits. At least you can try. (Experiences like these are one reason why I spent many pages on recognizing power dynamics in my book *The Sustainability Transformation*.)

And third, the older I get, the more I regret all those times when I felt forced — often by the strictures of some office I held or the perceived rules of play in a particular process — to exclude perfectly wonderful people from a very important conversation or process. Don't get me wrong: there are times when you do have to put a numerical limit around a specific gathering, because the dynamics of the gathering do not work at larger scale. And there are obviously times when you have to be discreet, or honor confidentiality. But there are plenty of times when these perceived boundaries are simply illusory. I often have to remind myself of a lesson I learned during my first collaborative sustainability project, Sustainable Seattle: inclusion breeds creativity. In that landmark process twenty years ago, for example, some of the best ideas for new indicators came from the youngest participants, who held no particular office or social portfolio — besides "student."[10]

So here is my message to you:

Take your guitar (or whatever the equivalent is for you) out of the case, and play it.

---

[10] Sustainable Seattle was a volunteer initiative that I co-founded in 1991 with other friends. Together we created the world's first set of sustainability indicators for a city, using a large-scale stakeholder engagement process. Sustainable Seattle was cited as a "Best Practice" by the United Nations and copied, or used as a reference point, by many other initiatives around the world. Remembering how several high school students contributed to our process in important ways still makes me happy.

Don't be naive about the fact that some people really will try to derail your plans. Be watchful, without being paranoid.

And as much as you possibly can, despite what I just said about some people not being trustworthy ... let people in. Let them participate. Let them create, contribute, collaborate.

Sustainability is for everyone.

The future of sustainability work

Someday we will all be able to stop working on sustainability, because sustainability will be fully and automatically integrated into nearly every aspect of our economies, societies, technologies, and personal lives.

But that "we" refers to humans in very general terms. It is probably not referring to us, here, now.

I have been a sustainability consultant for over twenty years. I fully expect that I will continue to consult on sustainability, in some form, for at least another twenty ... and probably all the way to my dying breath. To "consult" means simply, in the original Latin, to consider things carefully. To discuss them. To talk.

Looking ahead, we will certainly need to be talking about sustainability matters for the next several decades — regardless of whether we use that word or not. On the problem side, there will be climatic changes to adapt to, resource scarcity to manage, and continuing challenges with regard to preserving our planet's ecological integrity. There is a massive demographic transition to negotiate in the decades ahead, as the rich world becomes old, and the young world gets richer. There is the ever-present threat of conflict escalating into war, which will require ever more vigilance and diplomacy and preventative action, in an ever more crowded world. There is the continuing puzzle about what really makes people happy and satisfied with their lives, and how to provide that to them without wrecking this miraculous ball of life.

On the solution side, there are so many innovations that need to be diffused, so many great pilot projects that need to be scaled up, so many industries in search of transformation, and so many "invisible sustainability" stories and case studies to be discovered — or created — and broadcast around the planet.

There is enough work remaining to be done to keep all of us, who choose to make sustainability part of our life's work, busy for a long time to come.

More importantly, there is so much work to do that we who consider ourselves "professionals" can never hope to do it ourselves. We need to recruit others. *Many* others. In every profession, in every walk of life.

Yes, we will certainly need more sustainability professionals. But we will also need countless more sustainability "amateurs," people who work on promoting awareness and action from whatever regular position they are in, simply because they care.

Will professional sustainability work in the future be different from what we do now? Of course it will. Looking back twenty-five years (I started working in this field in 1988), I am amazed at how things have changed. Concepts like linking sustainability to change agentry had not yet been born. (I was fortunate to have a hand in introducing the concept of being a "sustainability change agent".) "Education for Sustainable Development" was still "Environmental Education." Corporate reporting had not even begun. There were certainly no standards, guidelines, or clear "Planetary Boundaries" defined and laid out for all to use. There were no sustainability graduate programs, training certificates, or master classes.

Now, we have hundreds or even thousands of these tools, concepts, and programs. More such useful tools and concepts are being developed every year as well. So are thousands of new sustainability professionals, schooled and skilled in the process of accelerating positive, transformative change.

And these new facts create the conditions for a new way of doing sustainability. For the foreseeable future — though of course, the future is mostly not foreseeable — I believe that sustainability work will be about scaling up, reaching out, deepening, broadening, engaging, including, mainstreaming.

Yes, the technical side of sustainability will continue to advance. We will need every good tool and trick we can devise. But the real challenge will be in bringing sustainability to more and more people, and getting them involved in the process of visioning, planning, and implementing transformation.

The real challenge, going forward, is to make sustainability less special, less different. More normal, more natural. Even something to build parties around! This is happening already, but we need to do it faster, just as fast as possible. This is why I am adopting this new motto for my work, and sharing it with you, and asking you to think about it with me.

So, please join me in a dialogue about this motto — about what it means, and about what it suggests we might do, to make the transformation we need happen more quickly.

Sustainability is for everyone.

Want to continue the conversation?

Please join the dialogue at this website/blog:

http://sforeveryone.wordpress.com

About the Author

Alan AtKisson was trained in philosophy, science, and the humanities at Tulane University, New Orleans, USA, and Oxford University, UK. Upon leaving university in 1981, he was selected a Henry Luce Scholar, and was sent to Malaysia to work for a year as a therapist for heroin addicts (he was 21 at the time). Returning to the US, he became a musician and songwriter in New York City, helped start a women's clothing design company, and worked as the administrator for an international peace organization, before starting his own magazine in 1988.

After one issue, he moved to Seattle and was hired as the managing editor of *In Context* magazine, a pioneering journal of sustainability issues, founded by Robert and Diane Gilman. In that position (and later as executive editor of the magazine), Alan became friends with many of the other early pioneers in sustainability work, including Donella Meadows, lead author of the 1972 classic *The Limits to Growth*. In 1992, Donella invited him to join the Balaton Group, an international network of sustainability thinkers and doers. That same year, he began consulting on sustainability and speaking at national and international conferences, based on his volunteer work with the ground-breaking initiative Sustainable Seattle and on the tools he had begun to develop for promoting sustainability change agentry.

Over twenty years later, having established an international network of small sustainability enterprises (AtKisson Group, ISIS Academy, and others); published several books (including *Believing Cassandra* and *The Sustainability Transformation*); and held several other leadership positions (including president of the Balaton Group and executive director of the Earth Charter Initiative), Alan AtKisson was elected into the Sustainability Hall of Fame™, in 2013, by the International Society of Sustainability Professionals.

For More Information

www.AtKisson.com

The website of the global AtKisson Group network
Consulting, research, and communication services

www.ISISAcademy.com

Our international professional development program
Master Classes, skill-building workshops, internal training

www.AlanAtKisson.com

Alan AtKisson's personal website / blog *"Words and Music"*

http://Pyramid2030.org

An international, volunteer-driven campaign to involve people in
the process of creating Sustainable Development Goals

http://sforeveryone.wordpress.com

The website for dialogue around this book

Made in the USA
Middletown, DE
12 January 2015